Al Jaffee's

SNAPPY ANSWERS to STUPID QUESTIONS

WRITTEN and ILLUSTRATED BY
AL JAFFEE

edited by ALBERT B. FELDSTEIN

WARNER BOOKS

A Warner Communications Company

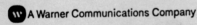

❧Dedication❧

To myself, without whose inspired and tireless efforts this book would not have been possible.

FOREWORD

"Mr. Allen wishes to acknowledge receipt of an advance copy of 'MAD's Al Jaffee Spews Out Snappy Answers To Stupid Questions'. Immediately after reading it, he and Mrs. Allen left on a well-deserved vacation."

DONNA ZINK
Secretary to
STEVE ALLEN

"Al Jaffee is a close and dear friend. One of the rare few one is privileged to know in his lifetime. His engaging wit, his fertile mind and his personable manner, makes each moment in his presence a moment to be cherished and re-called time and again.

"He is the personification of all that we, in his field, should hope to be and it is my fervent wish that someday it will show up in his work."

JOHNNY HART
Creator of B.C. and
THE WIZARD OF ID

"This is a very neat book. Seldom have I seen lines so equi-distant from each other. But this is not surprising, since the author is a very neat person. He is also a very nice person who dresses well and is very interesting to talk to. I would particularly like to call your attention to page 96. It is not a bad page at all. In summing up, I would like to say in all honesty that this is perhaps the only book that Al Jaffee has ever written."

LARRY SIEGEL
Noted Satire Writer
Co-Author:
THE MAD SHOW

"Stupid questions, indeed! Where would world history be without them? Suppose Noah had never asked: 'Think it'll rain?' Suppose Sir Walter Raleigh hadn't asked some Indian: 'Smoking a cigarette . . . or is your tongue on fire?' Or what if a fellow dogface in a desert dive hadn't asked Goliath: 'Getting stoned, big boy?' "

ALLEN SAUNDERS
Writer of MARY WORTH
and STEVE ROPER

"Me and my family have been fans of AL JAFFEE'S SNAPPY ANSWERS for years. Ever since they first came out we have been users of Al Jaffee's Snappy Answers. And now, our two year old son who has just turned to solid foods is using Al Jaffee's Snappy Answers. We have found that Al Jaffee's Snappy Answers last longer, wear longer and are easier to use than most snappy answers. They are particularly good in the morning at breakfast time with cream and sugar on them. What do I win?"

> EARLE DOUD
> Creator and Producer:
> "The First Family,"
> "Welcome To The LBJ
> Ranch," and other
> long-paying albums

"Having known AL JAFFEE (as he is jovially referred to by his intimates) ever since those halcyon days when we produced countless, capricious comic books together, I can do naught but heap the most glowing praise upon his pointy little head.

"This man, this creative titan, this Al Jaffee who walks among us, has a record which few can equal. Never, within human memory, has he precipitated a global war, committed genocide, or been incarcerated for jay-walking."

> STAN "Spiderman" LEE
> Editor: Marvel Comics
> Group

"Already, the top movie companies are bidding for the screen rights. As is, it would make a good shooting script for Michelangelo Antonioni. I see the lovely Faye Dunaway cast as 'Snappy.' "

> JERRY DE FUCCIO
> **MAD's** Night Watchman

"As the Editor of **MAD** Magazine, I have worked with many talented humor writers and comic artists over the years, helping them to develop their craft and watching them reach the full measure of their potential. As for Al Jaffee, all I can say is I'm still working with him."

> AL FELDSTEIN
> Editor
> **MAD** Magazine

9

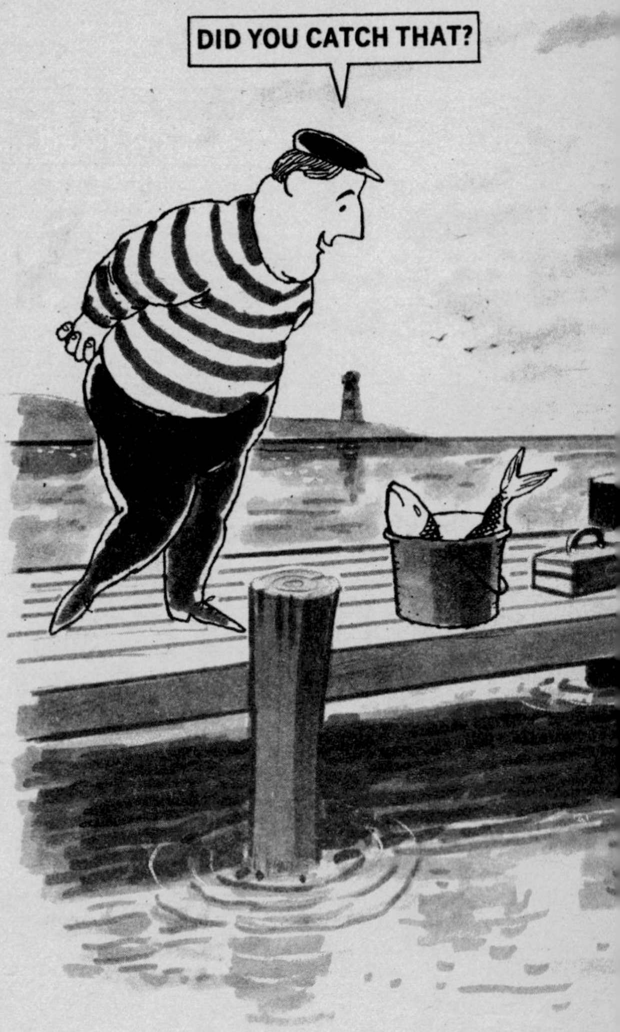
DID YOU CATCH THAT?

No, I talked him into **giving himself up.**
No, I was sitting here **minding my own business** when the crazy thing **jumped into my pail.**
No, it's a **plastic model** to get people like **you** to start **fascinating conversations.**
No it's the sittingnext tome fish.

17

THE GREAT
"SNAPPY ANSWERS
TO STUPID QUESTIONS"
MURDER MYSTERY

22

28

MORE
"SNAPPY ANSWERS
TO STUPID QUESTIONS"

31

35

"SNAPPY ANSWERS
TO STUPID QUESTIONS"
GOES WEST

STILL MORE
"SNAPPY ANSWERS
TO STUPID QUESTIONS"

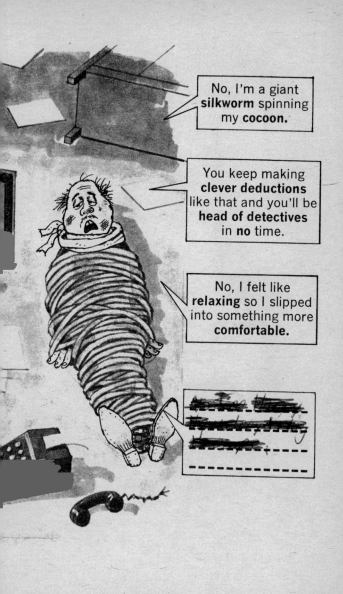

No, I'm a giant **silkworm** spinning my **cocoon**.

You keep making **clever deductions** like that and you'll be **head of detectives** in **no** time.

No, I felt like **relaxing** so I slipped into something more **comfortable**.

53

No, I got a **ride home** in a **water truck.**

No, I'm **practicing** to be a **water sprinkler.**

No, I'm **drenched** with **liquid sunshine.**

No I
Ta take
the suer
home

57

A
"SNAPPY ANSWER
TO SOME
STUPID QUESTIONS"
THAT BACKFIRED

BACK TO
THOSE PLAIN (YECCH)
"SNAPPY ANSWERS
TO STUPID QUESTIONS"

AN
OUT OF THIS WORLD
SNAPPY ANSWER
TO A STUPID QUESTION

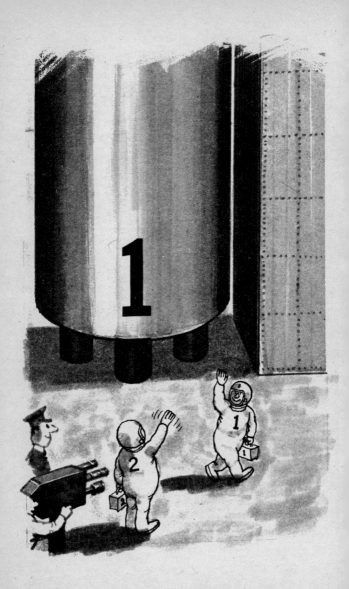

BACK TO
STILL MORE (YECCH)
"SNAPPY ANSWERS
TO STUPID QUESTIONS"

106

No, I'm studying the **cloud formations** here in our **basement.**

No, I'm **rehearsing** for my part as a **dragon** in the **school play.**

No, I'm just **sending messages** to an old **Indian friend.**

A ROMANTIC "SNAPPY ANSWERS TO STUPID QUESTIONS" LOVE STORY

ONCE AGAIN,
LET'S RETURN TO
STILL MORE (YECCH)
"SNAPPY ANSWERS
TO STUPID QUESTIONS"

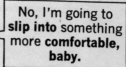

WHAT ARE YOU GUYS TRYING TO DO, MAKE TROUBLE?
DOWN WITH
STOP THE

127

"A SNAPPY ANSWER
TO A STUPID QUESTION"
BECAUSE IT IS THERE.

THROUGH HISTORY WITH "SNAPPY ANSWERS TO STUPID QUESTIONS"

140

STINGING COMEBACKS TO "SNAPPY ANSWERS TO STUPID QUESTIONS"

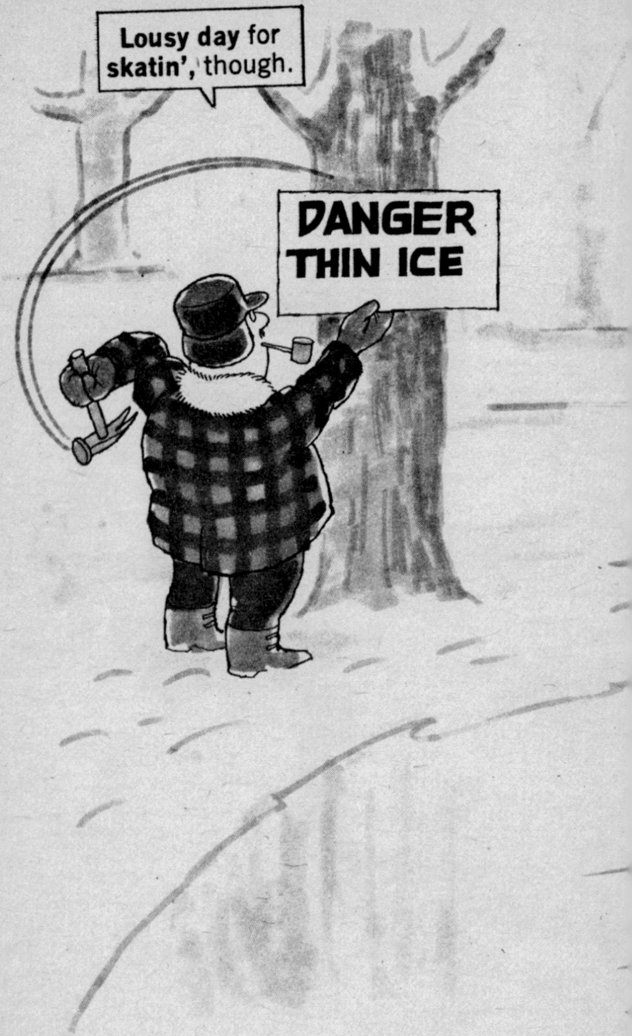
Lousy day for skatin', though.
DANGER THIN ICE

161

162

164

SOME VERY UNLIKELY
"SNAPPY ANSWERS
TO STUPID QUESTIONS"

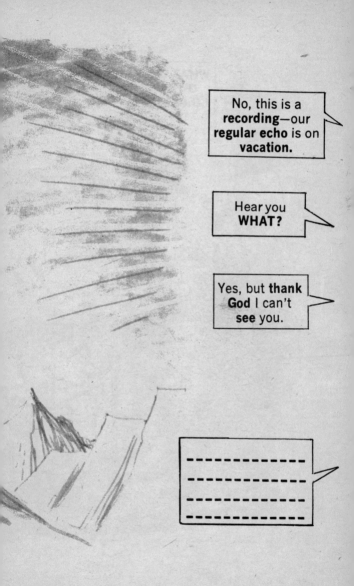

To the fact that I **haven't died yet.**

To **heavy drinking, wild partying, chain smoking,** and a number of things I can't mention in **mixed company.**

To **not asking stupid questions.**

AT LAST! THE LAST OF THE PLAIN (YECCH) "SNAPPY ANSWERS TO STUPID QUESTIONS"

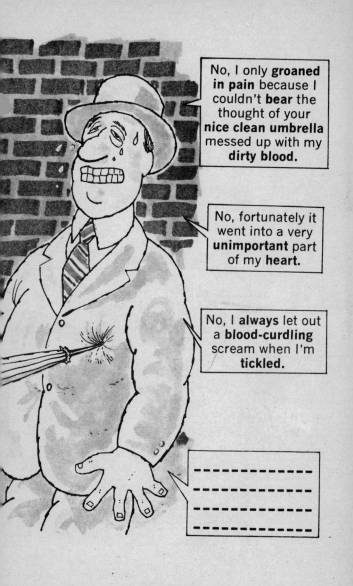

No, I only **groaned in pain** because I couldn't **bear** the thought of your **nice clean umbrella** messed up with my **dirty blood.**

No, fortunately it went into a very **unimportant** part of my **heart.**

No, I **always** let out a **blood-curdling** scream when I'm **tickled.**

_ _ _ _ _ _ _ _ _ _ _ _ _
_ _ _ _ _ _ _ _ _ _ _ _ _
_ _ _ _ _ _ _ _ _ _ _ _ _
_ _ _ _ _ _ _ _ _ _ _ _ _

179

181

183

A HAPPY ENDING TO A "SNAPPY ANSWER TO A STUPID QUESTION"

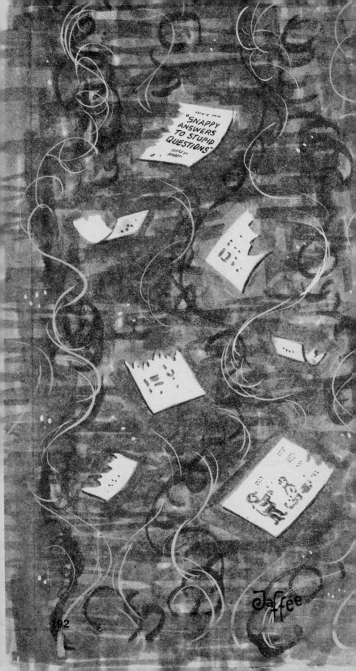